The Adventures of Molz Ammu the Aama

Written by

Susan Kokura

Illustrated by

Frank Passaretti

DEDICATION

To my parents who always stood by me no matter what and for making me work at the Waldwick public library, my husband Mattson for motivating me to publish this book, and my children Mason and Owen. To my amazing family and friends and to every human being I have ever met for helping me become who I am today. And to all the dreamers to never stop dreaming, nothing is impossible!

ON A PARTICULARLY HOT DAY IN KERALA,
MOLZ AND HER AMMACHI DECIDED TO GO
FOR A WALK BY THE PERIYAR RIVER.

"LOOK AMMACHI! AN AAMA!" GIGGLED MOLZ
AS SHE POINTED TO A SMILING TURTLE BY
THE RIVER BANK. "CAN I TAKE HER HOME?"
HER GRANDMOTHER SMILED AND ASKED,
"WHAT WILL YOU NAME HER?"
"AMMU," SAID MOLZ CONFIDENTLY. "AMMU
THE AAMA."
MOLZ GENTLY SCOOPED UP THE YOUNG
TURTLE AND SHE AND HER GRANDMOTHER
BEGAN BACK HOME.

IT DIDN'T TAKE LONG FOR MOLZ AND AMMU
TO BECOME BEST FRIENDS. THEY DID
EVERYTHING TOGETHER. THEY EVEN PLAYED
DRESS-UP! ONE DAY, MOLZ DRESSED AMMU IN
A SARI. SHE THOUGHT IT MADE THE LITTLE
AAMA LOOK VERY DIGNIFIED.

MOLZ WAS SO HAPPY TO HAVE A FRIEND TO SPEND THE LONG SUMMER DAYS WITH. THEY LOVED TO FLOAT PAPER BOATS IN THE RIVER.

THEY EVEN TRIED TO HELP AMMACHI COOK IN THE KITCHEN. MOLZ AND AMMU HAD A WONDERFUL TIME, BUT AMMACHI WAS NOT SO SURE THAT A TURTLE MADE A GOOD COOK.

MOLZ LOVED AMMU VERY MUCH. THEY WERE
VERY HAPPY.
BUT ONE DAY, MOLZ CAME HOME AND COULD
NOT FIND AMMU ANYWHERE.

SHE LOOKED EVERYWHERE.
MOLZ BECAME VERY SAD AND SHE BEGAN TO
CRY.

AMMACHI HEARD MOLZ CRYING AND
CONSOLED HER WITH A GENTLE HUG.
"I CAN'T FIND AMMU," SOBBED MOLZ.
AMMACHI KISSED HER FOREHEAD AND SAID
SOFTLY, "AMMU WILL NOT BE ABLE TO PLAY
WITH YOU ANYMORE."

"WHY NOT?" QUESTIONED MOLZ.
AMMACHI TOOK A DEEP BREATH AND
EXPLAINED THAT THE LITTLE AAMA HAD DIED
THAT MORNING.
MOLZ HUGGED HER GRANDMOTHER VERY
TIGHTLY AND CRIED.
"AMMU WILL LIVE FOREVER IN YOUR
MEMORIES," SAID AMMACHI. "AS LONG AS YOU
REMEMBER THE GOOD TIMES YOU HAD WITH
HER, SHE WILL NEVER BE FAR FROM YOU."

MOLZ DID REMEMBER THE ADVENTURES SHE
HAD WITH AMMU. THE MEMORIES MADE MOLZ
FEEL WARM INSIDE. MUCH TO HER SURPRISE,
SHE FOUND HERSELF SMILING THROUGH HER
TEARS.
AS THE DAYS PASSED, MOLZ BEGAN TO FEEL
BETTER. THE SADNESS DIDN'T GO AWAY
COMPLETELY, BUT THE MEMORIES OF AMMU
THE AAMA FILLED MOLZ WITH HAPPINESS.

THE TIME THAT MOLZ HAD SPEND WITH AMMU MAY NOT HAVE LASTED FOREVER, BUT THE GREAT MEMORIES WOULD PROVE TO LAST A LIFETIME.

39516748R00017

Made in the USA
Middletown, DE
17 January 2017